DUBLIN IN THE

1960s

Independent Archives

DUBLIN IN THE
1960s

SELECTED AND EDITED BY MICHAEL HINCH
INTRODUCTION BY DERMOT BOLGER

MERCIER PRESS
IRISH PUBLISHER – IRISH STORY

MERCIER PRESS

Cork

www.mercierpress.ie

© Independent Newspapers Ireland Ltd, 2016

© Introduction: Dermot Bolger, 2016

ISBN: 978 1 78117 466 1

10 9 8 7 6 5 4 3 2 1

A CIP record for this title is available from the British Library

Printed and bound in the EU.

Contents

Introduction

Dermot Bolger

One of my earliest childhood memories from the 1960s involves a bus being in a collision near Finglas. Passengers clambered off to sit on the footpath or huddle in groups, companionably offering around cigarettes. Their mood reflected annoyance at being delayed rather than any deep shock. But this atmosphere was electrified by the arrival of a photographer from the *Irish Independent* newspaper.

In a frisson of excitement, dazed passengers tried to make themselves look injured and those passengers merely inconvenienced produced combs to make themselves presentable. Previously the accident was a mundane annoyance: suddenly it was transformed by being newsworthy.

Passengers knew their photos would appear in the *Irish Independent* or *Evening Herald*, making them a part of the tapestry of daily news these papers relayed. Neighbours would eagerly ask them about it. Their photos would be cut out and posted to siblings abroad. Back then there was no Facebook. News was relayed by telegram or long-distance calls placed through an operator.

An *Irish Independent* photograph transformed any moment out of the ordinary. It wove additional glamour into attending a dance in Power's Hotel or the ballroom in Clerys department store. It gave recognition to a woman being evicted from her home on Swifts Row.

Glamorous young couples always attended the Trinity Ball; an elderly man lovingly pinned flowers to his wife's dress on a wedding anniversary; and Dubliners helped neighbours affected by a house fire. But these everyday events only became news when a newspaper photographer arrived; when printing presses whirled on Middle Abbey Street; and when newsboys implored passers-by to purchase the newspapers in which such everyday moments were rendered wondrous.

The 1960s was a fascinating decade of change in Irish life. Its first hint began in 1959 when Seán Lemass finally prised power from a reluctant, nearly blind Éamon de Valera and started to impose his new vision of Ireland. RTÉ Television encapsulated this modernity, and vivid pictures here reveal the build-up to its first broadcast on New Year's Eve 1961. De Valera's speech that night brimmed with foreboding about the changes television might usher in, but the people captured in the pages of this fascinating chronicle of 1960s Dublin were generally eager to embrace change.

Some figures here, like the cheerful Drumcondra/Glasnevin Old Folks Committee about to embark on a day trip to Bray, look like they belong to the 1940s. But a clamour of change infects other photos that capture the excitement of The Beatles playing Dublin in 1963: rioting teenagers overcome with exhilaration at being close to their heroes.

The pleasure of such a cornucopia of photographs of Dublin life is that it doesn't try to be a precise historical chronicle of how Dublin changed in that period. Historians can afford such overviews but newspaper folk are chained to tight deadlines, with the public eager for news of any specific day. This book will fascinate anyone interested in how the 1960s unfolded in Dublin. Here are the internationally famous: a glamorous Audrey Hepburn arriving in 1964 with no reference to her estranged father living in Dublin, Marlene Dietrich, Bing Crosby and David Niven.

Here, too, are a generation of artists who transformed how we saw ourselves: a young John B. Keane holding his son Billy, and The Dubliners embarking on a musical odyssey that lasted half a century. We see the old make way for the new – sometimes in planned demolitions, like the curtain coming down on the Queen's Theatre, and sometimes in unplanned demolitions, like when Nelson's head, sword and accoutrements rained down over O'Connell Street in 1966.

But this book is not only about public figures and events. A newspaper breathes in the aura of a city and reflects its readers' lives. De Valera once evoked an Ireland 'satisfied with frugal comfort'. But under Lemass, materialism was no longer a sin, entry into the EEC was a priority and – although the tortuous process took several decades – old shibboleths began to be swept away.

We see the start of the journey to today's Gay Pride marches in the photo of a mother and children kneeling in Marlborough Street for a Corpus Christi parade. This transformation would probably have seemed unimaginable to many of the people pictured here, but every person formed part of that journey – be they children playing outside the newly built Ballymun towers or models at Switzers' fashion show.

We see one way of life vanishing – exemplified by street traders hawking their wares in Moore Street – and a new Dublin emerge. Luckily for us, *Irish Independent* photographers were there to capture everyday moments and snatch them from time. These photographs form a people's history of our capital city. They chronicle a population busily getting on with life before rushing out to buy the next day's newspaper and see their lives reflected back in it. While capturing a vanished city, this book allows us to revisit those times, in images that remain as vibrant as on the day they were taken.

The City's Landscape

A view down Dublin's most iconic thoroughfare, O'Connell Street, towards O'Connell Bridge, taken on 27 September 1960. The monument to William Smith O'Brien, one of the leaders of the Young Irelanders Rebellion of 1848, can be seen on the left of the image. Beyond that the statue of Daniel O'Connell, 'The Great Liberator', is also visible.

As busy then as it is now, O'Connell Street is filled with the afternoon bustle of vehicles and people hurrying about their business. In the middle of the street the queue is building at the caravan selling tickets for Chipperfield's Circus. It is parked beside the CIÉ enquiries booth. In a sight that is still familiar today, queues for the buses fill the pavement on the far side of the road.

O'Connell Bridge teems with traffic and pedestrians, as the Daniel O'Connell monument stands proudly at the entrance to the street named after him. Designed and sculpted by John Henry Foley, the monument was unveiled to an enormous crowd in 1882.

Above: A view of the old Metropole cinema on a foggy, near-deserted O'Connell Street on 27 December 1961. Walt Disney's *101 Dalmations* was the film showing that week – in Technicolor, no less. The cinema closed in 1972 and a Penneys department store now stands in its place. Beside it is the GPO, probably Dublin's best-known building.

Right: The Monument Bakery and Café on O'Connell Street was part of the Monument Creameries chain established by Seamus Ryan. The chain was named in honour of the monument of Charles Stewart Parnell near this premises. At its height Monument Creameries had thirty-three outlets. A member of Fianna Fáil, Seamus was elected to the Seanad in December 1931. His career in politics was cut short by his untimely death in 1933 aged just thirty-eight. At the time of his death, the *Irish Independent* described him as 'displaying such acumen that he built up one of the most extensive businesses in Dublin'. The Creameries went into liquidation in 1966.

14

Above: The slushy remnants of a blizzard lie on the junction of O'Connell Street and Lower Abbey Street. The statue commemorating Sir John Gray, the proprietor of *The Freeman's Journal* newspaper, is visible in the centre. The Tylers shoe shop in the background was part of a chain that was a fixture in Dublin from the 1880s until it was taken over by ShoeZone in 1986.

Right: The Charles Stewart Parnell monument, photographed on a gloriously sunny 11 August 1964. A garda directs traffic in the right foreground. The fifty-seven-foot-high obelisk was created by the Irish-American sculptor Augustus Saint-Gaudens and unveiled at the junction of O'Connell Street and Parnell Street in 1911. The National Bank building in the background appears to be getting a facelift. This bank was started by Daniel O'Connell in 1835 and was absorbed by the Bank of Ireland in 1966.

Some things never change, as this image of gridlock on O'Connell Street shows. In the background looms Nelson's Pillar. The now pedestrianised area in the centre of the street was once a popular car parking area.

Cars weren't the only way to get around the city in the 1960s, as evidenced here, where two CIÉ workers drive onto O'Connell Street from Bachelor's Walk on a scooter.

Bicycles were also very popular, as this photo of rush hour traffic at the corner of Lower Abbey Street and O'Connell Street demonstrates.

Sunlight catches the buildings at the northern end of O'Connell Bridge, captured from Burgh Quay on 5 December 1962, as a calm-looking River Liffey streams past.

Above: Without the help of the traffic lights that can be found at the junction today, pedestrians bravely cross the always busy junction between D'Olier Street and O'Connell Bridge, while in the background, traffic builds on Aston Quay on 17 April 1964. The barrels in the middle ground appear to be part of traffic control measures.

Right: The rainy weather doesn't seem to bother this man, as he walks nonchalantly along the footpath on the corner of Westmoreland Street and Aston Quay, newspaper in hand. A row of public telephone boxes line up on the street corner, with one person sheltering between them from the rain. Sadly these telephone boxes, which were once such a common sight, have now disappeared from the city's streets.

A garda signals for a pedestrian to wait for the traffic to clear at the meeting point between D'Olier Street and Westmoreland Street. Behind the garda is the Lafayette building, built for the Liverpool and Lancashire Insurance Company in the 1890s and home in the 1960s to John Purcell Ltd, a tobacco importer and cigarette supplier.

Palace Street on an overcast day in December 1961. A glimpse of the lower yard of Dublin Castle is visible through the gated entrance. The AIB building on the left, designed by Sir Thomas Deane, has been a bank since it was built in the late nineteenth century to house the Munster and Leinster Bank.

Liberty Hall under construction on 17 August 1964. The new head-
quarters of the Services, Industrial, Professional and Technical Union
(SIPTU), it was built to replace the old building on the site, which
had been declared unsafe and was demolished in 1958. Neither the
old man reading the newspaper nor the seagull seem particularly
interested in the construction.

The recently completed Liberty Hall building seen from the Liffey in 1965. It stood at 195 feet, making it the tallest storeyed building in Ireland at the time.

Sparse traffic motors along Winetavern Street on 21 February 1964. The dome of the Four Courts can be seen rising above the rooftops further along the street. The derelict terrace seen on the left of the image was torn down in the early 1970s.

Ryan's Pub on Haddington Road in Beggars Bush occupies a site rich with history. It witnessed the battle of Northumberland Road and Haddington Road in 1916, which raged just fifty metres from the site of Ryan's. Until 1988, when the building was restored, bullet holes from that battle could be seen in the side wall of the pub. The site was sold to the Office of Public Works in 1967, but came back into the Ryan family's possession in 1988.

Above: A view of the Dublin Corporation-run Davitt House flats in Drimnagh. Children can be seen to the right, playing in the nice weather, while a woman hangs bedsheets on the clothes line in the centre of the yard.

Right: Children play on a roundabout outside one of the Ballymun tower blocks on a cold and overcast day in 1968. There were seven fifteen-storey tower blocks built in the 1960s to deal with Dublin's rising population. Each one was named after a leader of the 1916 Easter Rising: Patrick Pearse, James Connolly, Éamonn Ceannt, Thomas MacDonagh, Thomas Clarke, Joseph Plunkett and Seán MacDermott. All of these flats have now been demolished, the last, Joseph Plunkett Tower, in 2015.

A young man steers a horse-drawn cart through an autumnal, leaf-carpeted St Stephen's Green on 27 September 1960.

A father and son walk hand-in-hand along the canal at Charleville Mall, North Strand, on a beautiful late-summer's day in August 1964.

Moore Street's market is said to be Dublin's oldest food market, and is a famous landmark on the northside of the city. Here we see traders and customers alike milling about stalls that contain apples, potatoes and other fruit and vegetables. Nortons, a china and Delft pottery merchant, and Hanlon's fish shop can also be seen on the left side of the street.

The hustle and bustle of the Moore Street open air market captured on
27 October 1961. The fish stall in the forefront of the image appears to
be doing a thriving trade.

One of the Moore Street traders, Mrs Talbot, holds up a batch of bananas for sale. Mrs Talbot, like many of the traders, worked for decades at the market. Given the traders' propensity to continue working well into old age, an honorary title came to be given to the market's oldest trader – that of 'Queen' of Moore Street.

An ornate row of Georgian houses on Fitzwilliam Square, captured on
a clear and crisp December day in 1961.

The state funeral of W. T. Cosgrave moving through Rathfarnham on a wet day in November 1965. When the Irish Free State came into being in 1922, Cosgrave became its first prime minister, called the president of the Executive Council. He led Ireland through some of the most turbulent years of its history, and later became the first leader of Fine Gael. He is buried in Goldenbridge Cemetery in Inchicore.

Above: The white building on Ellis Quay is the site of the old Phoenix cinema. Opened in 1912, it proved to be very popular in this part of the city until its closure in 1958, after which the lower storey was converted into shops. Jaymac Importers was mentioned in a Dáil debate of 16 November 1961 about new companies and it apparently assembled ballpoint pens from imported components.

Right: The Plaza cinema, situated at the junction of Dorset Street Upper and Granby Row. Originally built in 1789 as a chapel, the building was converted into a cinema in 1911. *The Unforgiven*, which was showing, was a 1960 western directed by John Huston. The cinema closed in 1981 and sadly the building was demolished in 2005. A Maldron hotel now occupies the spot where the Plaza once stood.

The Destruction of Nelson's Pillar

Nelson's Pillar was blown up in the early hours of the morning of 8 March 1966 by a small republican faction. On the right is the CIÉ information kiosk. Its clocks, which were stopped by the force of the blast, show the exact time of the explosion, 1.32 a.m.

Nelson's Pillar in all its glory before the explosion. The 121-foot-tall monument to British Admiral Horatio Lord Nelson was completed in 1809 and towered over O'Connell Street for more than 150 years. In this image Nelson watches impassively as the Cardinal Legate Grégoire-Pierre Agagianian, a representative of Pope John XXIII, and his escort travel towards Áras an Uachtaráin for a meeting with President de Valera on 17 June 1961. By some accounts, over 100,000 people lined the route to welcome him.

Members of the emergency services struggle to lift Nelson's head out of the rubble. A group of students later stole the head from a Dublin Corporation lock-up. Over the next while it appeared in the window of a London antique shop, on stage with The Dubliners and even on Killiney Beach during a photo-shoot for women's clothing, before being recovered by the authorities. It is now displayed in the Gilbert Library on Pearse Street.

Six days after the explosion, on 14 March, the army destroyed what remained of the pillar in a controlled explosion. This image of the explosion was captured from nearby Henry Street. The *Irish Independent* of that day reported: 'Crowds watched from behind barricades of sandbags as an 80 lb. explosive charge was detonated to send the 50 feet high column toppling from its 30 feet high plinth. The stump went up in a huge blast that sent blue and white flame scorching out over O'Connell Street just before the column came crashing down in a dense cloud of white smoke, dust and tons of masonry.'

Above: Crowds gather to view the aftermath of the army's final destruction of the pillar.

Right: The so-called 'controlled' explosion wasn't quite so controlled. Gardaí were hurriedly placed on guard over gaping shop windows in Henry Street, O'Connell Street and Talbot Street. A burglar alarm set off by the blast clanged out over the scene of destruction where citizens milled round with faces covered with handkerchiefs to keep out the dust and smoke. The *Irish Independent* noted that 'rocks were hurled as far as fifty yards away on either side of O'Connell Street.'

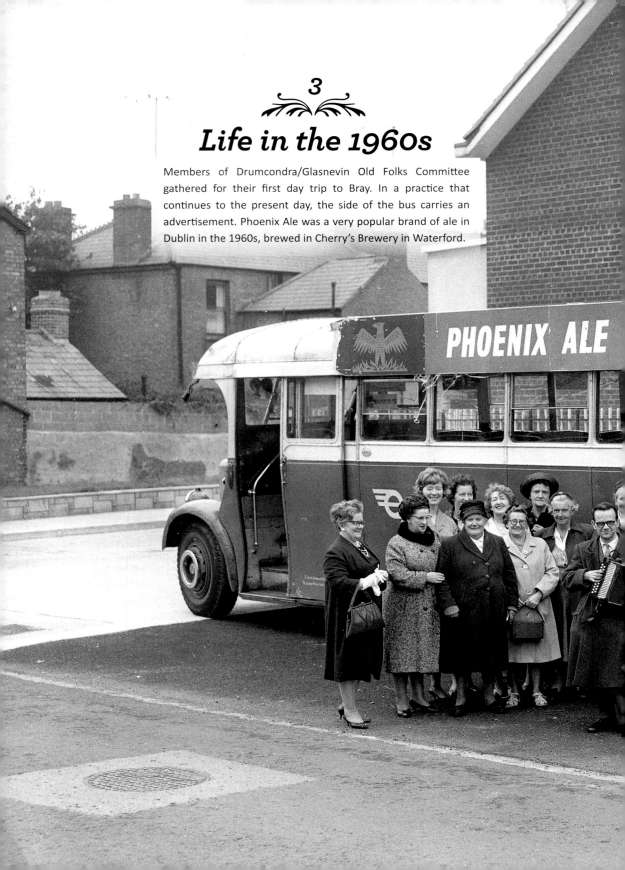

3

Life in the 1960s

Members of Drumcondra/Glasnevin Old Folks Committee gathered for their first day trip to Bray. In a practice that continues to the present day, the side of the bus carries an advertisement. Phoenix Ale was a very popular brand of ale in Dublin in the 1960s, brewed in Cherry's Brewery in Waterford.

PHOENIX ALE

Brothers Michael and Rorke Ryan from Rathfarnham sit on a
1923 Matchless 980cc. They rode this motorcycle combination
in the Veteran Motorcycle Run to Butlin's Holiday Camp in
Mosney, Co. Meath, from St Stephen's Green in August 1964.

Rockin' in the Good Old Time – quite literally. A dressed-up Ken Harold from North Circular Road and Mary Cheevers of Finglas sit on their 1916 Triumph 500cc before the start of the Veteran Motorcycle Run.

Above: At a reception for the US Surgeon General Luther Terry on 19 August 1964, Mrs J. M. R. Grainger (*left*) and Mrs M. L. Conalty share a drink and a joke. Terry, who was selected for the job by John F. Kennedy, was a vocal opponent of smoking. He set up the Surgeon General's Advisory Committee on Smoking and Health and in early 1964 it released a groundbreaking report that outlined how smoking was hazardous to health.

Left: Taking advantage of the good weather, Nell and Alice Ringrose take in the sun in St Stephen's Green on 14 August 1964. The Green is still a popular place to relax on a sunny day in Dublin.

Then, as now, a popular way to spend an evening out was to go to a traditional music session. Here, Monah Parkes, Cathy O'Malley, Joan Bowen and Nuala Doyle are enjoying the International Students Night Ballad Session on 12 August 1964. The Wolfe Tones performed on the night.

Dances were also an important part of the social life of young people in the 1960s. In this image Deirdre Whelan from North Circular Road and James O'Toole of Dorset Avenue arrive at the Kingsway Ballroom, Parnell Square on 17 August 1964, ready for some dancing. Such venues would have had live music, and it was in the Kingsway that a young Dickie Rock was discovered.

Above: Breda Monaghan at the National Ballroom, Parnell Square. The National was a major venue for dances in its heyday, playing host to all the top showbands of the era. It closed its doors in 1989.

Left: Patty O'Gorman from Stradbally, Co. Laois, and Brendan Dowdall of Co. Wexford at the Donegal Association Dance held in the National Ballroom on 17 August 1964.

Ann Cullinane at The Claremen's Dance in the National Ballroom in 1964.

Dancing at the Monday Night Social in the Irish Club, Parnell Square were Frank Murphy of Blackwater, and Mary Whitmore of Gorey, both in Co. Wexford. The Monday Night Social was held in August 1964.

Above: Young women at the Garda Basketball Club Dance in the Clerys Ballroom in September 1964. Clerys Ballroom was in Clerys department store, a famous institution on O'Connell Street. At one stage dances were held every night, with a full-time orchestra employed. The ballroom closed its doors in the 1970s because of competition from other forms of entertainment. Clerys itself survived as a well-known retail outlet until its closure in June 2015.

Right: Lillian Morrisey enjoying herself at the Clerys Ballroom on 14 August 1964. Big hair was the order of the day and the beehive hairstyle that Lillian sports was created in the 1960s by renowned hairdresser Vidal Sassoon.

Above: Margarita Vasconcellos and Mary Hogan at the Fermanagh Association Dance in Clerys.

Left: Mrs Michael Keegan and Mrs John Johnston also attended the Fermanagh Association Dance in the Clerys Ballroom. Their bouffant style of hair was another common sight in the 1960s, and their choice may have been influenced by Jackie Kennedy, a style icon of the time who favoured this look.

Elsie Whelan at the PAM Dance in the CIÉ Club in Inchicore on 14 August 1964.

A smiling Marie Keogh also attended the PAM Dance in the CIÉ Club that night.

Above: Perhaps considered an unusual event today, sixty years ago the double wedding was a common occurrence. Many couples opted to celebrate with another couple close to them, often family members or good friends. Vera Lennon and her sister Miriam celebrated with a joint wedding on 10 September 1964. The grooms, Alo Doyle and Kevin Keyes, wore matching suits, while the brides carried matching bouquets.

Right: Mrs Phil Sharpe of 33 Herberton Park, Rialto. Voted 'Ireland's Most Glamorous Granny', she is seen here with her two-year-old grandson, Raymond Byrne, on 11 September 1964.

Mr and Mrs Doyle of 22 Clanbrassil Street Upper on the occasion of their fifty-fifth wedding anniversary on 10 June 1964. Mr Doyle is pictured here pinning a rose to his smiling wife's lapel.

With the flower pinned on, the Doyles are ready for their formal portrait.

Above: Women at work: staff at the new Philips Factory in Finglas, which was officially opened in September 1964. The ladies pictured are Olive Harold, Maura Barry, Maureen Farrell, Monica Green, Ann Barry and Susan Young.

Right: Nora Lever, public relations officer of the Dublin Society for Prevention of Cruelty to Animals, smiles as she poses with two of her feline charges on 29 April 1964. Established in 1840, the DSPCA was based on Grand Canal Quay until it moved to Rathfarnham in 1990.

Mrs Rilty, retiring postmistress of Clondalkin, on 29 May 1964, stands at the counter she had worked behind for many years, with her daughters Josephine on the left and Mrs Dympna O'Brien on the right.

Cookery demonstrator Ann Russell and her assistant Elizabeth Goster judging bread at the 12th Annual Show of Our Lady's Horticultural Society in Drimnagh on 15 August 1964.

Above: The interior of the Clerys department store on 6 October 1961. The staff, all dressed in black, wait behind the counter to serve customers or answer queries. Freedex was a British manufacturer that specialised in leather handbags.

Right: Clerys wasn't Dublin's only large retail outlet. Founded in 1843, Arnotts is Ireland's oldest department store. Here Grace O'Shaughnessy models a tweed coat from their winter collection directly outside the store on Henry Street on 8 October 1962.

Another shopping institution in Dublin in the 1960s was Switzers (now Brown Thomas) on Grafton Street. This shot was taken during their autumn fashion show on 15 September 1964.

Switzers, which opened its doors in 1838, was always a byword for luxury, and its clientele would find only the most up-to-date fashions in its elegant store.

Bagging a bargain: while his mother is preoccupied by the discounted boys' windcheaters during the first day of the 'January' sales on 27 December 1961, something more interesting has caught the eye of this little boy.

Of course, once you'd made your purchase, you had to have somewhere to show it off. Veronica Fitzpatrick, Petra Reilly and Marion Koppler look their best at the Adelaide Dinner in Power's Hotel, Kildare Street on 30 May 1964.

Another elegant event at which to look your best was the
Trinity Ball. Marie Cook, Rosa Dunn and Maria Jose Pendas
pose here in their elegant dresses at the 1964 ball on 30 May.

This stylish couple, Mr and Mrs John Coker, also attended the Trinity Ball that year. First held in 1959, the annual ball has become a permanent fixture of the university year.

More elegant gowns can be seen in this picture from a fashion show held in Leixlip Castle on 31 May 1964. Several hundred people attended to see the spring/summer collection of Parisian designer Miguel Ferreras. *Left to right*: Martine Roma, Pascale Leruste, Francoise Alt, The Hon. Desmond Guinness, Liliane Samsoviei and Michelle O'Leary.

People sit – some more captivated than others – while a model in a fashionable coat and hat descends the staircase at the show. This event very nearly didn't take place, as the plane carrying the ninety-piece collection from Paris developed engine trouble and was stranded in London. Luckily five models who had flown from Paris specially for the show had brought twenty-five pieces in their baggage, which at least gave those attending a glimpse of Ferreras' collection.

Above: Not all life was glamorous balls and fashion shows. Pictured here are (*left to right*) Mrs Gunning, Mrs Coyle, Mrs O'Brien and Mrs Waldron, all residents of the Dublin Corporation flats in Davitt House, Drimnagh, on 2 May 1964. Thirty-six families occupied these flats, with close to sixty children, yet the only clothes-drying facilities provided by the Corporation are shown in the picture. Each mother could have the use of only one line for one day a week, and even that was only in theory – if you did not 'book' a line by 6 a.m. you had no chance of drying clothes until the next week.

Right: A resolute and seemingly unperturbed Mrs Lennox of Swifts Row sits outside on 14 August 1964, surrounded by her household items. She had been evicted shortly before this photograph was taken.

On 12 August 1964 a fire ripped through 49 Marlborough Street. The next day a garda stands outside, most likely to ensure that no one enters the badly damaged building. A small group has also gathered to stare at the fire-gutted house.

The fire left the three ladies who lived there homeless, including eighty-year-old Elizabeth Maher (*second from right*) and her sister, Mary, who were both treated in hospital. They are shown here with Ita Gibson (*left*), daughter of the proprietor of St Mary's Guest House, 63 Marlborough Street, who accommodated the three ladies after the fire. Mary McGrath (*second from left*) was also evacuated from her home.

The 1960s witnessed some social unrest. On an overcast day, 11 May 1966, the Irish Creamery Milk Suppliers Association (ICMSA) held a picket outside Leinster House. They had put forward a proposal for a two-tier price system for milk production and the rejection of this proposal prompted many weeks of protesting. On this particular day 120 picketing farmers were arrested for their part in the protest, with a total of 452 charged throughout its course. They were charged with taking part in picketing within half a mile of Leinster House while the Dáil was in session. All the convicted protesters were handed either a fine or a one-month prison term.

A queue of mostly women and children smile up towards the photographer and raise empty jars and bottles as they wait for a milk collection. Milk shortages were a problem for Dubliners throughout the ICMSA strike.

Eoin O'Mahony points the way as he marches at the head of a group of
UCD students parading to Lower Fitzwilliam Street in December 1962.
They were protesting against the ESB's plans to demolish sixteen Georgian houses on the street to make way for a modern office block, con-
sidering this a crime against Dublin's heritage. On arrival, the protesters
laid 'mourning wreaths' outside Nos 16 and 22.

Despite the protests, the Fianna Fáil government of the time, which included then Minister for Justice Charles Haughey, seen here sauntering into Dublin Airport in May 1964, allowed the destruction to go ahead. The controversial office block stretched for a full kilometre from the corner of Lower Mount Street to the corner of Lower Leeson Street.

Éamon de Valera had resigned as taoiseach and leader of Fianna Fáil in 1959, and was quickly elected president in June that year, a position he would hold until 1973. A veteran of the Easter Rising and War of Independence, he is seen here on 3 April 1962, with his aide-de-camp Colonel S. Brennan in the background, arriving at Kilmainham Gaol, where he had been imprisoned after his capture during the Rising. Also shown are Mr S. Dowling (*left*) and Mr J. J. Brennan (*right*).

President de Valera on his eightieth birthday, 14 October 1962, with his wife, Sinéad, and members of his family outside Áras an Uachtaráin.

Above: On 2 September 1962 the new Howth lifeboat *A.M.T.* was named by President de Valera's wife, Sinéad. The name *A.M.T.* was in honour of those who provided the £35,500 needed for the lifeboat: Mr Edward Auston of New Barnet, Hertfordshire, Miss Jessie Muhlhauser of Carshalton, Surrey and Mr A. Toon of Shilton, Leicester.

Right: Captain the Honourable V. M. Wyndham-Quin, deputy chairman of the RNLI, presents Sinéad de Valera with a miniature silver model of a lifeboat at the ceremony.

Then, as today, sport, and especially Gaelic games, played an important role in the free time of Ireland's citizens. In 1960 the Down team brought the Sam Maguire Cup on a visit to President de Valera at Áras an Uachtaráin following their historic win over Kerry in the All-Ireland Football Final. Down was the first team from the six counties of Northern Ireland to win an All-Ireland.

President de Valera watches as Tipperary vice-captain Tony Wall clutches the McCarthy Cup. Tipperary had just defeated Wexford at Croke Park in the 1962 All-Ireland Hurling Final with a scoreline of Tipperary 3–10, Wexford 2–11. This was the first All-Ireland final broadcast live by Telefís Éireann.

Horses have long been an integral part of Irish life and the Royal Dublin Society (RDS) arena was developed to host equestrian events, including the annual Dublin Horse Show. In this picture Fergus McVeigh of Hollywood, Co. Wicklow (*left*), and Conor Lynn from Coleraine, Co. Derry, can be seen exercising their horses at the arena in the summer of 1963.

In 1961 the Irish civilian show-jumping team undertook a European tour in which they swept up a total of twenty-six prizes, including five red rosettes, in Belgium, Holland and Switzerland. Here Colonel J. J. Lewis, chairman of the Show Jumping Association of Ireland (*centre*) is pictured with members of the team after they arrived back in Dublin following their success. *Left to right*: Mr L. Fitzpatrick, Tommy Brennan, Seamus Hayes and Brian MacNicholl.

Binoculars at the ready: the crowd at Fairyhouse Racecourse watches with anticipation as a race unfolds. Fairyhouse, although in Co. Meath, was a popular day out for Dublin racegoers. Some people, like the man in the right background, did whatever was necessary to gain a vantage point.

The legendary racehorse Arkle with his owner, the Duchess of Westminster; his trainer, Tom Dreaper, and jockey Pat Taaffe, a Dubliner. Named after the mountain bordering the Duchess of Westminster's Sutherland estate in Scotland, Arkle won three Cheltenham Gold Cups as well as a host of other top prizes before his career was cut short by injury.

Another way to get involved in the excitement of the races was through the Irish Hospitals' Sweepstakes draw. The sweepstakes was a national lottery established by the government in the 1930s as a means of funding the country's hospitals due to the shortfall in public finances. Many of the entries came from Irish emigrants in the United States and the United Kingdom. Tickets were put into large rotating barrels, manned by nurses in their bright white uniforms. The nurses would draw out the tickets, each one assigned to a horse taking part in various races, including the Grand National. The very first sweepstake took place at the Mansion House in Dublin in 1939, later moving to the RDS. These images show the draw underway in Ballsbridge on 13 March 1964.

Jockey Tommy Wade with his horse Dundrum on 21 August 1962. Tommy Wade and Dundrum were champion showjumpers who enjoyed much success in the late 1950s and early 1960s, including winning the Grand Prix at the Dublin Horse Show in 1963. Aside from their great success, the pair stood apart from the competition due to Dundrum's small stature. At just fifteen hands high he was much smaller than most and yet went on to become one of the era's best-known showjumpers.

Ronnie Delany is a member of an exclusive club in Ireland — he is one of a handful of Irish people to have won a gold medal at the Olympics. On 17 July 1961, at the Clonliffe Harriers two-day meet at Santry, he was part of an Irish 4 x 1 mile relay team that faced a New Zealand team which included the 1960 Rome Olympics 800-metre champion, Peter Snell. Snell's team broke a world record in this relay, coming in at 16 minutes and 23.8 seconds. The picture shows Delany (*left*) with Snell (*right*) and George Kerr of the West Indies.

Before any of today's golfing superstars were even a twinkle in their parents' eyes, Dubliner Joe Carr had built a reputation as one of Ireland's greatest golfers. He is shown here on 25 April 1962, after winning the West of Ireland Golf Cup for the fourth time in a row, with a treasure trove of silverware from throughout his golfing career. With him are his children: Gerry, John, Joe, Sibeal, and Roddy. In 1967 Joe would be the first Irishman to make the cut and play in the Masters Tournament in America.

Spectators at the City of Dublin Open Championship at Ashbrook Lawn Tennis Club, Rathgar, on 15 August 1964. The club, which was founded in 1922, is still going strong today. It ran the championship from 1964 to 1970, and in 1967 hosted the Irish Open.

A new form of entertainment emerged in the 1960s that would soon supersede all others – television. In this image sections of the first Irish television transmitter mast are prepared for erection on Kippure Mountain on the Dublin/Wicklow border. The building and raising of the mast were completed during the summer of 1961.

With the Kippure mast completed, Telefís Éireann was ready for its first broadcast. The television service started broadcasting on New Year's Eve 1961. Here we can see the setting up of lighting on the Gresham Hotel, O'Connell Street, ahead of the first transmission. The station was launched by President de Valera, with addresses from Taoiseach Seán Lemass and Primate of All Ireland Cardinal John D'Alton. There was also a live broadcast from the Gresham, where cameras filmed the public dancing outside in the snow.

Above: A view of the busy TV newsroom inside the Montrose studio. The purpose-built studios have housed RTÉ in Donnybrook, Dublin 4, since 1961.

Left: The television service proved enormously popular, as evidenced here by the group gathered around the TV, watching a live benediction service. Television quickly became an important and powerful force in Irish culture. Topics that had often been deemed controversial, such as contraception or abortion, were now able to be discussed in front of a national audience.

Another technological advance that affected people in the 1960s was the growing commercialisation of air travel, which allowed more people to travel further afield than ever before. In this picture Conor Cruise O'Brien, a noted Irish politician, academic and writer – often nicknamed 'The Cruiser' – arrives into Dublin Airport from New York in 1961.

Members of 'Ireland on Parade', pictured at Dublin Airport before their departure to the USA in September 1964. Ireland on Parade comprised a group of 100 performers from the Garda Band, singers Patrick O'Hagan and Mary Sheridan, the Tara Boys Band and the O'Connell Girl Pipers, who toured fifty-nine US cities, including Boston, Chicago and Philadelphia, for two months. This unlikely troupe was, at the time, the largest ever party to leave the country on one flight.

Large groups travelled in the opposite direction as well. Pictured here are members of the Éire Society of Boston with President Éamon de Valera outside Áras an Uachtaráin. On his right stands Harry Weldon, the tour director. The Éire Society of Boston was established in 1937, by a group of eighty-two adults fresh from a sixteen-lecture crash-course in Irish history presented by the Massachusetts Department of Education to promote knowledge of Irish culture in America.

With easier access to travel, events in Ireland began to take on a more international feel. In this picture are (*left to right*) Miss M. Kimiot from Greece, Mrs Varghese of India and Mrs Kaskassiades from Paris, attending a luncheon held in Dublin's Zoological Gardens on 17 September 1964. The event was held for the wives of delegates attending the Aviation Medical Conference nearby.

Also attending the luncheon at the Zoological Gardens were Mrs V. Johnstone from the UK, Mrs C. N. Lucas and Mrs Rigaud from France, Mrs B. Amirian, who was based in Ireland at the time, and Una Barry. They all look a little bemused by Mrs Amirian's decision to wear sunglasses indoors.

Renowned Irish dance teacher Lily Comerford, in her role as Director of the International Dancing Festival, checks the festival programme with West Indies dancer Beverley Lawson, at the Mansion House on 1 September 1964. Lily founded the Irish Folk Song and Dance Society and many dancers travelled to Ireland to perform in the international festival she organised.

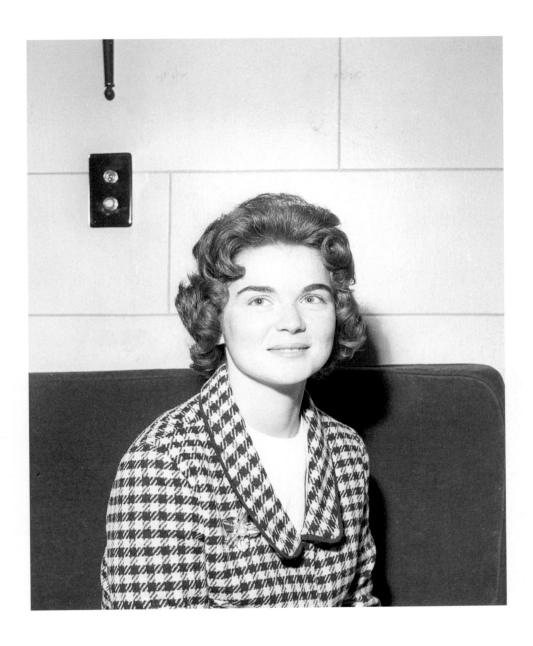

Miss Irish-America, Catherine Marren of Newark, New Jersey, on a visit to Ireland. She is pictured here at the Hibernian Hotel, Dawson Street, on 11 August 1964.

Another pageant winner who visited Ireland was Anne O'Regan, winner of the Portsmouth Irish Society Personality Contest. She is seen here chatting with Portsmouth Councillor Henrietta Brady on 13 August 1964 shortly after their arrival in Dublin. Winning the personality contest entitled Mrs O'Regan to a week's holiday in her native Dublin. The two women were put up in the Gresham Hotel. In the personality contest – the first to be held by the society – entrants were judged on their competence in Irish singing and dancing, as well as their personality, charm and beauty. Mrs O'Regan, formerly Anne Sheridan of Clonard Road, Crumlin, was home for the first time in eight years.

A more famous emigrant to be celebrated in this decade was James Joyce. On 16 June 1962, the fifty-fifth anniversary of Bloomsday, the Joyce Museum was opened. It was located in Sandycove, on Dublin's coastline, in a former Martello tower that had been part of the defence network built to protect Ireland from the threat of invasion by Napoleon's forces in the early nineteenth century.

A large crowd gathered for the auspicious occasion, including relatives and acquaintances of Joyce himself. At the time of opening, the museum contained personal belongings of the writer, manuscripts and a death mask of Joyce made in Zurich.

Sylvia Beach inaugurated the Joyce Museum, hoisting the Milesian banner – a blue flag with three crowns that features in the novel *Ulysses* – to mark the opening of the museum. Sylvia, pictured here (*left*) speaking to Mr N. Sheridan and the writer Mary Lavin, first published *Ulysses* in 1922 from her Paris-based bookshop, Shakespeare and Company. Joyce turned to her when he was unable to get an edition published in English-speaking countries.

4
Childhood

Happy youngsters cheer as they attend the Catholic Social
Welfare children's sports meeting, held at the play-centre,
Kylemore Road, Ballyfermot on 15 August 1964.

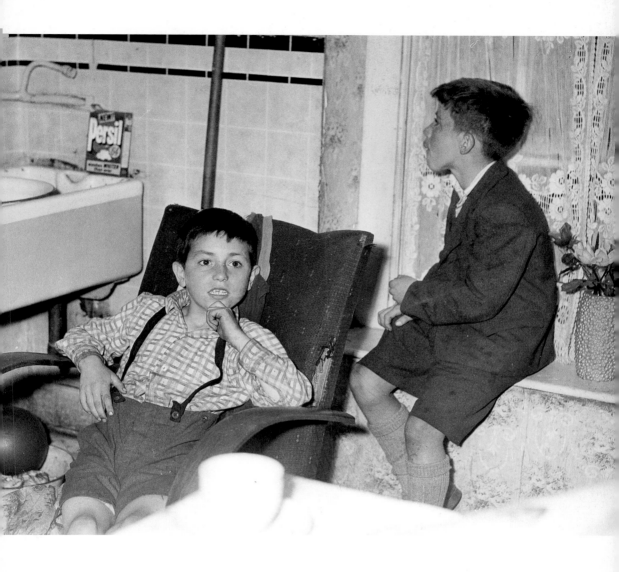

Above: Twelve-year-old Michael from Sheriff Street had to be rescued from the ledge of a high building by Dublin Fire Brigade while searching for pigeons. He is pictured with his brother, Anthony, on 13 August 1964.

Left: In contrast, twelve-year-old Patrick Flannery did the saving when he pulled a six-year-old boy from the Grand Canal on 8 June 1964, outside his home in Fatima Mansions, Rialto. Standing on a chair in order to reach the clothes line, he is drying his trousers after his courageous rescue.

A crowd of children queue for a swim in the Tara Street baths, eager to cool off in the warm weather. The baths were opened in 1885 and were well enough known to get a mention in James Joyce's *Ulysses*. The building was demolished in 1986 and the Markievicz Leisure Centre now stands on the site.

Above: Founded in 1883 in Scotland, the Boys Brigade's stated aim is 'the advancement of Christ's kingdom among boys and the promotion of habits of obedience, reverence, discipline, self-respect and all that tends towards a true Christian manliness'. Here the 22nd Dublin Company's annual inspection and display at Sandymount Church Hall is taking place on 14 April 1961. Some of the boys are undergoing a final check from their captain, Mr S. A. Evans. The pillbox hat the boys are wearing was part of the original uniform and was replaced later in the 1960s by a forage cap.

Left: Eamon Bradley of the Tara Boys Band was part of the 'Ireland on Parade' tour of America in 1964. He was chosen to help open and close each performance by raising and lowering the Irish and American flags. It was claimed that Eamon was the first of the new Irish republicans. He was born within three minutes of the official inauguration of the republic on 17 April 1949 – the first citizen under the new order, as far as is known.

Boys and girls pose for a group photo outside the church after their First Communion ceremony in June 1964. Some parents stand proudly at the back of the group.

Lord Mayor of Dublin Seán Moore talks to two seemingly unimpressed children in June 1964. Moore was the mayor from 1963–64.

A little girl helps a street cleaner with his work, watched by Moore.

Above: Excited students watch and some applaud at the Coláiste Mhuire prize-giving ceremony on 2 June 1963. This all-boys gaelcholáiste was founded in 1931 and was based in Parnell Square. It remained there until August 2003, when it moved to the Ratoath Road area of the city.

Right: Firm friends. Five Inter-Cert students pose outside a Georgian house in inner city Dublin on their way to school in 1964. Dressed in a formal and fashionable uniform emblazoned with their school's crest, knee-length skirts, and ties striped in the school's colours, they look fully prepared for the school day ahead.

Above: A lollipop man signals for school children to hurry across the pedestrian crossing on the North Strand in December 1961. A queue of traffic waits patiently for the children to cross.

Left (left to right): Alan Bray, Joseph Rankin, James Deegan and Christopher Furlong, who held a jumble sale in aid of 'Freedom from Hunger' in June 1964. They raised one pound and two shillings. The 'Freedom from Hunger' campaign was launched by the UN in 1960 to raise awareness of hunger and malnutrition around the world and to organise solutions to this at national and international levels.

Above: Children queue for a ride at a fair in Dublin. The excitement is clear on the little girl's face in the centre of the photo, but the parents' expressions aren't quite as enthusiastic. A merry-go-round operates in the background.

Right: A grand day out: children play in a puddle on a beach on the Dublin coastline as their doting grandmother watches on.

Generation games: what looks like three generations of the one family relax on a bench. Although the 1960s saw the advent of the collapsible stroller for babies, the style of pram seen here was still a common sight.

Student nurse Kathleen Naughton from Cork with two of her charges at the Children's Sunshine Home annual open day in Stillorgan on 19 May 1962. Set up in 1925 by Dr Ella Webb, the home provided residential care for children from tenements with acute rickets and later tuberculosis and congenital heart disease. It is now the LauraLynn Ireland's Children's Hospice.

Young jockeys line up at the RDS with saddles, bridles and horse-whips in hand. Above their heads, a sign points in the direction of the grand stand enclosure. These children were most likely attending the Dublin Horse Show, Ireland's largest annual equestrian event.

The next Dubliners? A very youthful band show off their skills on top of the *Independent* building in June 1964. One boy on the ledge is singing, while the other three boys play the tin whistle, the harmonica and, on the left, a melodica.

5
Celebrity Visits

Her Royal Highness Princess Grace of Monaco with her eldest daughter, Princess Caroline, leaving Dublin Airport to board a London-bound plane on 26 June 1961. While in Ireland Grace had visited the area in Mayo where her grandfather John Kelly had grown up before emigrating to Philadelphia.

Above: Dublin Airport was the portal to the rest of Ireland for many dignitaries. In this picture Princess Margaret and her husband, Lord Snowdon, are being escorted to their plane by J. F. Dempsey, General Manager of Aer Lingus (*far right*), at the end of a visit to Ireland in August 1962.

Right: As well as royalty, Hollywood also came calling. Actress Audrey Hepburn and her actor husband, Mel Ferrer, arrived at Dublin Airport for a weekend holiday on 14 August 1964. Hepburn said: 'This is my first visit to Ireland and I hope that friends are going to drive us through the countryside.'

Above: Esteemed actor and star of *My Fair Lady*, Rex Harrison (*left*), chats with Frankie Byrne (*centre*), Ireland's first ever agony aunt. She hosted RTÉ's *Dear Frankie*, which ran from 1963 to 1985. A warm and charismatic personality, she quickly became a household name, dispensing witty and warm advice while discussing people's personal lives and covering topics that would have been considered quite taboo at the time.

Left: Charlie Chaplin waves to the gathered media and fans as he arrives at Dublin Airport on a visit with his wife, Oona (daughter of the famous playwright Eugene O'Neill). Chaplain was a frequent visitor to Ireland, and holidayed in the country throughout the 1960s.

It's a wonderful day as film star James Stewart, the lead in classic movies such as *Rear Window* and *It's a Wonderful Life*, visits Áras an Uachtaráin on 2 August 1962. Between Stewart and President Éamon de Valera stands Stewart's wife, Gloria Hatrick McLean.

Sir Alec Guinness, star of *The Bridge on the River Kwai*, *The Ladykillers* and *Lawrence of Arabia*, speaks with Phyllis Ryan at the Eblana Theatre (in the basement of Busáras) on 23 June 1962. Ryan was an Irish actor and theatre producer known for championing the work of Irish writers. In 1934, at age fourteen, she had her debut on the stage of the Abbey, and by sixteen was a member of the company.

Peter O'Toole (*right*), with Marie Kean, Fred O'Donovan and Denis Carey, arriving into Dublin. O'Toole, Kean and Carey were due to perform in the Gaiety Theatre's production of *Juno and the Paycock* during Horse Show week in July 1966. O'Donovan was the producer of the play.

The actor and folk singer Burl Ives arriving at Dublin Airport in 1966. Probably best known for his Oscar-winning performance in *The Big Country*, Ives had two Irish grandmothers, whom he credited with giving him a love of Irish traditional songs. In the 1950s he released an album called *Songs of Ireland*.

Star of stage and screen Sir Ralph Richardson at the Russell Hotel, St Stephen's Green, on 22 August 1964.

Of course Ireland also had plenty of home-grown talent. Barry Fitzgerald, the Irish stage, film and television actor, starred in *The Quiet Man* and won the Oscar for Best Supporting Actor in 1945 for his role as Father Fitzgibbon in *Going My Way*. He has two stars on the Hollywood Walk of Fame.

Actor Milo O'Shea, star of the films *Ulysses* and *Barbarella*.

Marcella Grimes, a popular Dublin actress, who played a riot leader in the film *Young Cassidy*.

A gathering of actors on 17 March 1960. *Left to right*: Diane Aubrey, Pat O'Brien, Kenneth Connor MBE, Noel Purcell, Jill Adams and Leslie Phillips. Kenneth Connor was a British stage and screen actor. He is best remembered as a veteran cast member of the Carry On films, appearing in seventeen in total. He also appeared in 'Allo, 'Allo.

Film personalities Joe Lynch and Dominic Behan chat between
takes on 28 June 1960. Both were taking part in *Johnny Nobody*,
which was filmed at Ardmore Studios in Bray.

Actress Zsa Zsa Gabor smiles as she tries on an Aran cardigan in Dublin Airport during her visit to Ireland on 13 October 1961. Married nine times, she is known for many quotes, one of which is: 'A man in love is incomplete until he has married. Then he's finished.'

Actress Margaret Rutherford preparing to open the Pere Pire Christmas card sale outside Trinity College, with M. P. Stanfield, the organiser of the event, on 26 November 1961. Rutherford was best known for her role in the film adaptations of Oscar Wilde's *The Importance of Being Earnest* in 1952 and for playing the character of Miss Marple. She won an Oscar for Best Supporting Actress in Terence Rattigan's 1963 film *The V.I.P.s*, which also featured Elizabeth Taylor, Richard Burton and Maggie Smith.

The actor Arthur Kennedy shares a laugh with his wife, Mary, and daughter, Laurie, on their visit to Dublin on 25 August 1962. Kennedy was an American stage and film actor known for his versatility in supporting roles in film and his theatrical work, especially in the original productions of Arthur Miller's plays on Broadway.

Above: Film stars Alan Bates (*left*) and Laurence Harvey (*right*) pose with an Aer Lingus hostess at Dublin Airport in September 1962. Harvey was best known for his roles in *The Manchurian Candidate* and *Three Men in a Boat,* while Bates starred in *The Go-Between* and *Far from the Madding Crowd.*

Right: George Sanders, actor and star of *All About Eve* and *The Jungle Book*, attending the Curragh races on 27 June 1964.

David Niven, star of *Around the World in Eighty Days*, is warmly greeted as he arrives on 21 May 1966 to film scenes for *Casino Royale*.

John Huston, director of numerous films including *The Maltese Falcon* and *The African Queen*, *c.* 1964. Huston had moved to Ireland in 1952 and became an Irish citizen in 1964.

German-American actress and singer Marlene Dietrich being interviewed at Dublin Airport on 28 November 1966.

Bryan Forbes CBE signs an autograph for an air hostess on 15 March 1963. Forbes was an English film director, producer, screenwriter, actor and novelist. Some of his best-known work was *The Stepford Wives* of 1975, which he directed, and *The League of Gentlemen* in 1960 and *Only Two Can Play* in 1962, which he scripted.

Above (left to right): Actors Penny Chatterton, Ray Cox and the Tony Award-nominated Rosaleen Linehan enjoy themselves while attending an after-party following a production at the Abbey.

Right: Bing Crosby, the American singer and actor, visiting the Guinness Brewery in 1966. Crosby was one of the biggest selling recording artists of the twentieth century, selling over one billion records worldwide.

On 8 November 1962 British singer Helen Shapiro touched down in Dublin from Liverpool for a show at the iconic Adelphi Theatre on Middle Abbey Street. If the concert went well, theatre management had agreed to put on six shows a year of a similar calibre, so great expectation hung on this one-night-only performance. Shapiro's show must have been deemed a success as The Beatles played at the Adelphi the following year.

Ella Fitzgerald, the American jazz singer, arrived at Dublin Airport on 15 April 1964. This was her first professional visit to Ireland and she sang at two concerts in the Adelphi.

Pop singers Peter Asher and Gordon Waller, who made up the singing duo Peter and Gordon, signing autographs while surrounded by fans at the Dublin Intercontinental Hotel in Ballsbridge. They achieved fame in 1964 with the song 'A World Without Love' and had several subsequent hits in that era.

The Swinging Blue Jeans look to be all business on their arrival at Dublin Airport for a ten-day tour of Ireland in September 1964. This four-piece British Merseybeat band was best known for hits such as 'You're No Good', 'Hippy Hippy Shake' and 'Good Golly Miss Molly'.

Butch Moore finishes one more celebratory pint before bed. Moore was an Irish showband singer who shot to fame as Ireland's first ever Eurovision Song Contest representative in 1965. A huge hit, the song 'Walking the Streets in the Rain' secured sixth place in the competition. From 1960 to 1966 Moore toured with the successful Capitol Showband, performing in dance halls across Ireland. The group were regulars on television programmes like *The Showband Show*, as well as performing in London and the United States.

The Dubliners in 1966 (*left to right*): Ciarán Bourke, Ronnie Drew, unknown, John Sheahan, Barney McKenna and Luke Kelly. Founded in 1962 in Dublin, and originally called The Ronnie Drew Group, The Dubliners went on to become one of the most successful, and iconic, Irish bands of the twentieth century. In 1966 they released their third album, *Finnigan Wakes*.

The Wolfe Tones (*left to right*): Noel Nagle, Brian Warfield, Derek Warfield and Liam Courtney. Instruments at the ready, they are just about to go on for their performance at the International Students Night Ballad Session on 12 August 1964. The Warfield brothers and Nagle grew up together in the Inchicore area of Dublin, and formed the folk band in 1963. They went on to great national and international success with songs like 'My Heart is in Ireland' and their version of 'A Nation Once Again'.

The Clancy Brothers and Tommy Makem perform in front of a packed house in 1964. In that same year, almost one-third of all the albums sold in Ireland were Clancy Brothers and Tommy Makem records. Note the advertisement for the *Irish Independent* in the background: 'The paper with a punch!'

The Clipper Carlton Band on 4 June 1960. Standing (*left to right*):
Fergus O'Hagan, Hugo Quinn, Dom Shearer, Mick O'Hanlon and Terry
Logue. Seated (*left to right*): Victor Fleming, Hugh Tourish and Art
O'Hagan. Founded in the late 1940s, The Clippers are credited with
starting the whole showband craze in the late 1950s. Against the
staid, traditional approach of 'orchestras' at the time, which involved
mostly just sitting down and playing music, The Clipper Carlton Band
stood up, moved around and engaged with the dancing audience.

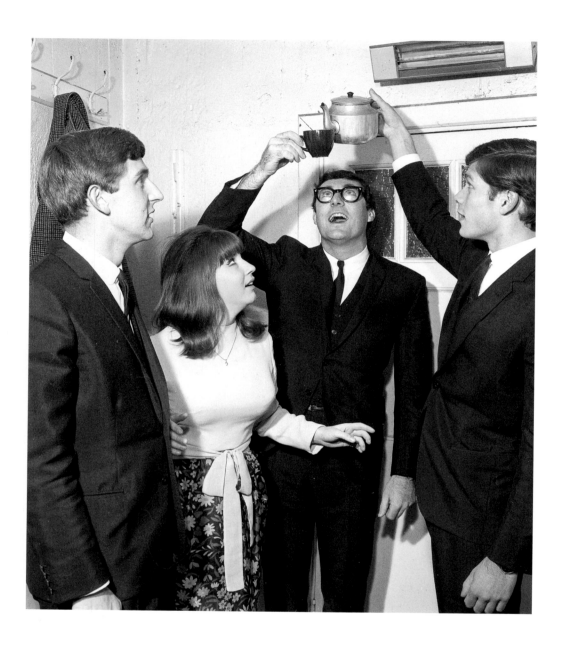

The Seekers (*left to right*: Bruce Woodley, Judith Durham, Athol Guy and Keith Potger) pour some tea in a comical fashion at the National Stadium on 20 November 1965. The Seekers were an Australian folk-influenced pop music group. Originally formed in 1962, they were the first Australian group to achieve major chart and sales success in the UK and US. Their biggest hits include 'Georgy Girl' and 'I'll Never Find Another You'.

Athol Guy enjoys a cigarette before The Seekers' performance at the National Stadium on Dublin's South Circular Road. Guy played the double bass for the band, and was characterised by his distinctive black, horn-rimmed glasses. He also, sometimes, acted as the group's compère.

A couple of heavyweights from the sporting world also visited Dublin during the sixties. In this picture, taken on 29 September 1964, Jack Doyle, the former Irish boxer, actor and accomplished tenor, admiringly squeezes the flexed biceps of Henry Cooper, the European and British heavyweight champion of the time.

President Éamon de Valera with the legendary boxer Joe Louis, outside Áras an Uachtaráin on 8 October 1966. Louis was the world heavyweight champion from 1937 to 1949 and is still considered one of the greatest heavyweights of all time. It was Kerry native Michael 'Butty' Sugrue who arranged for both Cooper and Lewis to tour Ireland. Sugrue later brought Muhammad Ali to fight in Croke Park in 1972.

Above: Irish author, critic and historian Ulick O'Connor enjoys the view overlooking Dublin on 9 April 1964.

Right: Artist Pauline Bewick at the Irish Exhibition of Living Art in the National College of Art on 11 August 1964.

Dublin-born Cornelius Ryan, author of *The Longest Day*, was in Eason & Son Ltd in November 1962 to autograph copies of his book. With him are former classmates from Synge Street Christian Brothers School.

Beatlemania

The Beatles performed a double bill on 7 November 1963 at the Adelphi Theatre on Middle Abbey Street, their first and only Irish show. This picture was taken during the first show of the double bill.

Above: As The Beatles arrived at the Adelphi, teenagers, mostly girls, rushed forward screaming. The fifteen gardaí who were present at the time managed – just about! – to hold them back.

Right: Already, even at this early point of the night, 'Beatlemania' was beginning to take hold. Teenagers screamed and cheered, while others – desperate to see their heroes – climbed a nearby parking sign. The first performance was due to begin at 6.30 p.m.

Before the show, the famous foursome (John Lennon, Paul McCartney, George Harrison and Ringo Starr) made sure to pose for pictures with fans on stage. Ringo even gave his drumsticks to the lucky fan nearest him.

Outside, gardaí struggled to hold back the ever-increasing crowds as they pressed forward towards the Adelphi's doors.

Gardaí lined both sides of the street in the vicinity of the theatre, desperate to keep order. Motorists were warned not to park their vehicles in the locality and most businesses shuttered their windows hours before the show started.

The fans, however, weren't too interested in keeping order.

Unaware of the chaos outside, The Beatles waited in the dressing
room of the theatre, their first performance about to begin.

194

Eager fans happy that they are finally about to be allowed inside the theatre.

Paul McCartney and George Harrison are shown here singing
on stage during the first performance.

Outside, more excited fans had already started to gather for the second show.

The heavily outnumbered gardaí continued to struggle to
keep things under control.

All semblance of control was lost outside the theatre as scuffles broke out and people fainted. At least a dozen young men were taken into custody.

A teenager carries his friend outside, after he fainted inside the theatre.

Amazing scenes were witnessed after the first show as 2,000 people emerged into the street, where hundreds were waiting to gain admission to the second show. In the crush, young women and children fared worst. According to a report in the *Irish Independent*: 'For a considerable time the crowds refused to move.'

When the curtain came down on the second show the band, still in stage clothes and make-up, ran down to the open door at the back of the theatre. Amid all the mayhem, the four Beatles were successfully smuggled into an Independent Newspapers van and driven off through the unsuspecting crowd to the Gresham Hotel.

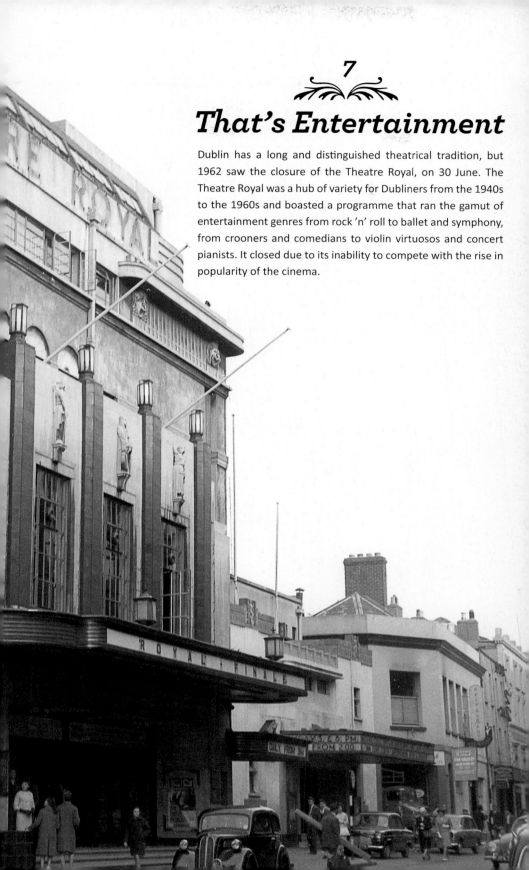

7
That's Entertainment

Dublin has a long and distinguished theatrical tradition, but 1962 saw the closure of the Theatre Royal, on 30 June. The Theatre Royal was a hub of variety for Dubliners from the 1940s to the 1960s and boasted a programme that ran the gamut of entertainment genres from rock 'n' roll to ballet and symphony, from crooners and comedians to violin virtuosos and concert pianists. It closed due to its inability to compete with the rise in popularity of the cinema.

Various staff and performers, including Jimmy Campbell (in the tuxedo) and Mickser Reid (*front row, right*) pose for a photograph outside the Theatre Royal before the final show. Veteran performer Campbell lamented on behalf of the city, saying 'Everyone is sorry to see the last of the Royal.'

Jimmy Campbell poses with Pauline Forbes, Dolores Murphy and Kay Condon ahead of the Theatre Royal's final show. Forbes was a guest performer on the bill for the final night. The Theatre Royal on Hawkins Street was the fourth reincarnation of the theatre, with the original site in Smock Alley dating back to 1662.

The final bill for the Theatre Royal was a triumphant celebration of the art of variety entertainment and featured esteemed performers including Noel Purcell, Joseph Locke, Jimmy O'Dea, Milo O'Shea, Cecil Sheridan and Jimmy Campbell. Tommy Dando, pictured next to a pipe organ, also performed, playing 'Keep Your Sunny Side Up' on the night.

Behind the scenes, performers Mickser Reid, Sean Mooney, Alice Dalgarno and Noel Purcell reminisce. They all, undoubtedly, had fond memories of the theatre.

Above: The Royalettes backstage at the Theatre Royal with performer Cecil Sheridan merrily stationed in the centre.

Right: The end of an era – some of the Royalettes finishing up after the show. The Theatre Royal was demolished in the weeks following closing night to make way for a new set of office blocks. The building that replaced it is known as Hawkins House, which became the home of the Department of Health and has often been voted 'the ugliest building in Dublin'. Hawkins House, in turn, is set to be demolished in the near future.

A portrait of actor Robert Brown in the Gaiety Theatre on 30 March 1962. Brown would later become famous for playing the role of M in a number of James Bond movies.

A portrait of actor Paul Rogers, also in the Gaiety Theatre on 30 March 1962.

The Olympia Theatre on Dame Street has hosted some famous faces in its time. In this picture (*left to right*) actor Cyril Cusack, actress Joan Plunkett and politician and Abbey Theatre managing director Ernest Blythe are deep in conversation on 17 March 1962. They were attending the twenty-first anniversary party for IMP Productions, a theatre production company. Most of the cast of IMP's very first production, *Private Lives*, attended, including Plunkett.

A packed hall. The Radio Éireann Symphony Orchestra with the St James's Gate Choral Society and O'Connell School Boys Choir rehearse in the Phoenix Hall on 12 December 1962. Phoenix Hall was in Dame Court and had previously been used by the Irish Hospitals' Sweepstakes before being adapted by Radio Éireann for its orchestra's concerts. The hall was small, with seating for an audience of just 400, but the concerts were all free.

'It's not just a pantomime, it's a Gaiety pantomime' has become a familiar catchphrase in the run-up to Christmas. The pantomime at the Gaiety Theatre on South KIng Street is a long-running tradition. In 1963 it was *Goldilocks and the Three Bears*. Here actors Jimmy O'Dea and Maureen Potter joke together ahead of the performance on 26 December 1963.

The actor Harry Brogan prepares for his appearance as Joxer in Sean O'Casey's *Juno and the Paycock* in the Abbey Theatre's 1964 production. The Abbey had a long history of producing O'Casey's plays. The first performance of one of his plays took place in the Abbey in 1923, when a production of *Shadow of a Gunman* was mounted.

Eileen O'Casey, Sean O'Casey's widow, with Denis Carey of the Dublin-based Sundrive Players theatre company. She was present for the group's production of O'Casey's play *Within the Gates* in 1964.

Not quite the London Palladium! A small crowd gathered on 1 February 1964 to watch a piano being lifted up to the first floor of Murray's pub (now the Ha'penny Inn) on Wellington Quay in Temple Bar, ahead of a performance by Josef Locke. Born in Derry, Locke was a hugely successful tenor in Britain in the 1940s and 1950s. He took part in five Royal Variety Performances in the 1950s in prestigious London venues in front of senior royalty. However, following issues with the taxman, he fled to Ireland in 1958 and, although he continued to perform, his career was never the same.

Bill Peel (*centre*) and Rick Bourke (*right*) marvel at Noel Purcell's short pigtail on 30 May 1964. Purcell was a prolific actor on stage and screen. Born in Dublin in 1900, he embarked on an acting career at the age of twelve and went on to appear in various stage productions, films and television shows, including the 1956 film *Moby Dick*.

John B. Keane and his son Billy, who was six years old
at the time, at the opening night of *The Year of the
Hiker* at the Gate Theatre, Parnell Square, on 18 August
1964. Actress Maire Hastings, who played the role of
Mary in the production, sits alongside them.

Actor Martin Dempsey, in costume, played the titular role of the hiker in Keane's play.

A night out with front-row seats at the Eblana Theatre for Mr and Mrs Keane on the left, of Donnybrook, and Mr and Mrs Dowling on 17 September 1964. The Eblana Theatre was situated in the basement of Busáras, Dublin's central bus station, and operated by Bus Éireann. It was open from 17 September 1959 until 1995. Run by Phyllis Ryan, it was home to her company Gemini Productions. Early works by the likes of Brian Friel, Tom Murphy and John B. Keane were premiered at the theatre.

Charles H. Schneer at the Dublin Theatre Festival with his daughter Lesley on 18 September 1964. Schneer was an American film producer and screenwriter, whose film credits included *Jason and the Argonauts*, released the previous year, and *Clash of the Titans*, released in 1981.

Bringing the curtain down. After a 1951 fire destroyed the original Abbey Theatre building, the company relocated to the Queen's Theatre on Pearse Street. What was intended to be a temporary visit in fact turned into a fifteen-year stretch. The final Abbey-produced performances at the Queen's were of *Never the Time and the Place* by Lennox Robinson and *The Irishwoman of the Year* by John Power. This signalled the end of an era for both the Abbey and the Queen's. Pictured (*left to right*) are P. Long, C. Bright, L. Scott, K. Bourke, T. Wakefield and J. Ellis.

Vincent Dowling applies make-up ahead of the last Abbey-produced performance at the Queen's Theatre on 9 July 1966.

On 18 July 1966, fifteen years to the day after fire destroyed the original Abbey Theatre, the new Abbey Theatre was opened on Lower Abbey Street. President Éamon de Valera attended the opening. He is talking to Abbey actress May Craig, while to the left Harry Brogan chats with Vincent Dowling.

Frank Aiken (*left*), the Minister for External Affairs at the time, also attended the opening.

The Queen's Theatre did not survive for long after the Abbey departed. The Happy Gang, a troupe of comics, singers and performers who regularly appeared at the theatre, can be seen here on closing night in 1969. They smile and wave to the crowd as the final curtain falls on the historic theatre. Demolition of the building began in January 1970 in what the *Irish Independent* described as the 'death knell of a great era in the world of Dublin theatre'.

8

The Big Freeze

Three boys with a sled trailing behind them walk up a hill in the Stepaside area of Dublin on 29 December 1962. Christmas that year in Ireland was marked by bitingly cold winds, treacherous snowy conditions and below freezing temperatures.

A snowy, near-deserted Middle Abbey Street during the height of the cold spell that spread across the country in winter 1962–63.

With sports fixtures cancelled, photographers covered the snow front. Brothers Frank (*left*) and Tony McGrath, *Independent* staff photographers, plod through the knee-deep snow near Tallaght to find the perfect shot.

Continuous snow made travel by car or plane incredibly dangerous, with motorists warned to take extreme care. Despite precautions, however, some vehicles still got caught by the conditions, such as these travellers trapped in a snow-drift near Templeogue on 29 December 1962.

The snow drifts were very difficult to walk through, but this man persevered, eager to return to his family. Or perhaps to get away from them?

Despite the hardships it caused, people still sought to make the best of the weather, such as these Dubliners who travelled to Phoenix Park to play in the snow.

Michael Mason from Kilternan and Joan Presch of Stepaside also
made sure to enjoy the snow as they rode a sled down a hill at
Stepaside on 29 December.

Waves of up to forty feet were reported along Dublin's coastline
and one woman was swept to her death at Dalkey Harbour. This
picture shows the rough seas at Howth pier.

On 30 December Dublin Airport ceased operations by
11 a.m., stranding 3,000 passengers due to travel back to the
United Kingdom, where blizzard conditions were also wreaking
havoc, claiming the lives of five people on 30 December alone.

Above: The country continued to suffer from the freezing temperatures into the New Year and by 3 January 1963 food supplies in mountain and village areas of Counties Dublin and Wicklow were running dangerously low. The *Irish Independent* arranged special airlift deliveries of hot food and supplies. Preparations for one such emergency run can be seen here, with supplies being loaded at Dublin Airport on 5 January.

Right: Anthony Osborne, a resident of the Dublin mountains area, whose family was struggling with food shortages, receives food parcels. The house behind him is nearly lost beneath the snow.

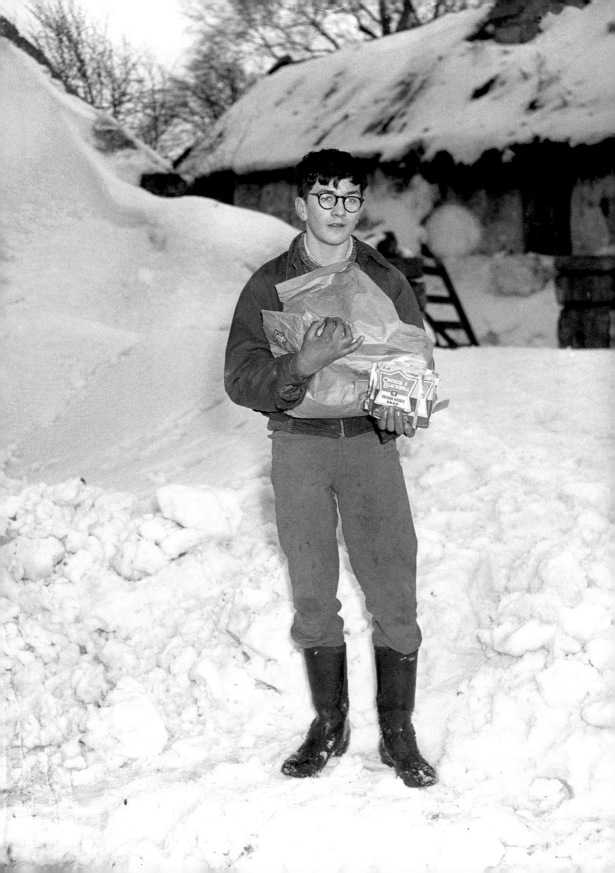

Members of An Óige unloading food parcels from an *Irish Independent* truck on 5 January 1963 at Valleymount, Co. Wicklow. Residents in Valleymount were without light for three days when the electricity failed.

The same members of An Óige wave as they make their way through the snow drifts from Valleymount to Granmore with food parcels.

By 14 January the front pages proclaimed that 'All Europe Freezes' as what was becoming known as 'the great freeze' extended its icy grip to the French Riviera, with temperatures above freezing only to be found on the Mediterranean island of Corsica. Back in Dublin, icy conditions prevailed and it was reported that 'in at least one Dublin public house stout froze in the bottles'.

Members of the Irish Mountaineering Club set out from
Blessington with supplies for families in the mountains, on 5
January 1963.

In what was the coldest winter of the twentieth century,
the snow and freezing conditions continued until early March,
when the thaw finally came.

9
Parades

Vintage tractors on their way to a parade hold up traffic on O'Connell Street in view of the Metropole cinema in 1964. The GPO can also be seen in the background, as can part of a still-intact Nelson's Pillar. The front tractor was built by the International Harvester Company, an American manufacturer of farming machinery started in 1902.

Down memory lane: a tram returns to the streets of
Dublin for the annual St Patrick's Day parade in March
1964. The city trams had ceased operation in 1949. The
tram is covered in advertisements for Player's cigarettes,
presumably because, as it says on the side of the tram, it
passed the Player's factory on its original route between
Dolphin's Barn and Glasnevin.

Religious parades were also part of the annual calendar. On 31 May 1964 parishioners from all over the city came together to celebrate the feast of Corpus Christi, otherwise known as the feast of the Holy Eucharist. Hundreds took part in this solemn procession, which in this picture is moving along Marlborough Street.

A lady and four children kneel on the footpath outside Perry's hairdressers on Marlborough Street, waiting for the Corpus Christi parade to pass. They all have their hands clasped in prayer.

Corpus Christi is Latin for 'body of Christ'. On the right some members of the Irish Army are accompanying the procession. An altar boy on the far left appears to be ruining the solemn mood, however, as he shares a joke with the boy alongside him.

Members of the men's sodality of St Columba's Church, Iona Road, taking part in the procession in Dublin on 31 May 1964.

Newly confirmed girls in Holy Communion dresses also took part in the Corpus Christi parade. Flags and bunting decorated the route of the procession.

In 1960 the UN issued a call for troops for a peacekeeping mission to the Congo, as discord rippled through the newly independent country. The Irish Army responded enthusiastically for what was its first major overseas operation since the foundation of the Irish state. That year 700 troops were deployed from the hurriedly formed 32nd Battalion. One month later the 33rd departed to join them. More followed thereafter, including the troops of A and B Companies, some of whom can be seen here boarding their plane for the Congo at Baldonnel on 26 May 1961.

One of the US Air Force Globemaster aircraft which arrived at Dublin Airport on 21 September 1961 to take supplies to the Irish troops in the Congo. Upon arriving in the African nation, it quickly became apparent that the Irish Army was woefully under-prepared and lacking in resources, starting with what was on their backs. Made from traditional 'bull's wool', their uniforms were suffocatingly heavy in the tropical climate.

Relieved soldiers on their return from the Congo, delighted to be back on home soil. Irish troops would be deployed in the Congo for four long years. The last troops left on 30 June 1964 when the UN mission there was wound up.

Army children Michael and Bernard White and T. Appleby
patiently await their fathers' arrival at Clancy Barracks on their
return from the Congo on 24 November 1961.

A medal presentation at McKee Barracks near Phoenix Park. The medals are being presented by Taoiseach Seán Lemass to soldiers who had served in the Congo, where they patrolled a portion of land several times larger than the whole of Ireland.

Not all the soldiers Ireland sent were lucky enough to make it home alive. This picture is from the funeral of Dubliners Lieutenant Paddy Riordan and Sergeant Paddy Mulcahy, and Private Andy Wickham from Campile, Co. Wexford. These three members of A Company, 36th Battalion, were killed, along with several other Irish soldiers, at the Battle of the Tunnel on the outskirts of Elizabethville, a Congolese city the army successfully saved from a military force of the Katangan gendarmes. Escorting the remains to Glasnevin Cemetery on 4 January 1961 are (*from right*) Lieutenants Ray Roche, Jack Duggan and Tom Kempton.

The funeral of Trooper Anthony Browne of the 33rd Battalion, one of the victims of the Niemba ambush of November 1960. The Niemba massacre occurred just four months into the mission. Nine Irish troops were killed when Baluba tribesmen ambushed an eleven-man patrol, with only two surviving the attack. Also being buried was Corporal Michael Nolan of the 35th Battalion, who was killed in action in September 1961. His body was brought back with Trooper Browne's remains.

Veterans of the 1916 Easter Rising take part in its fiftieth anniversary commemorations. Events took place throughout March and April in many places, such as outside the GPO on O'Connell Street and at Kilmainham Gaol.

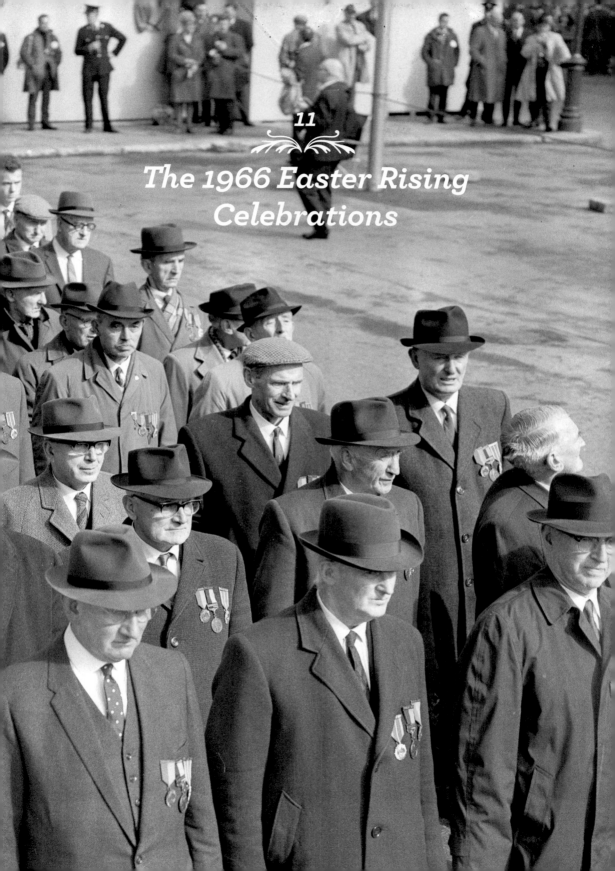

The 1966 Easter Rising Celebrations

Dubliner Helena Molony at the celebrations. An active participant in the Rising, Molony was with the Irish Citizen Army contingent which occupied Dublin City Hall. When the British Army stormed the building she was arrested and was one of only five women involved in the Rising to be interned in England. As well as being a prominent republican, Molony was also a staunch feminist and socialist. She died just a year after these commemorations, in 1967.

Above: Veterans of the Rising with their families outside Kilmainham Gaol for the 1916 commemoration, April 1966. Most of the men executed following the Rising were put to death by firing squad in this gaol.

Overleaf: The Irish Army marches along O'Connell Street in the military parade on Easter Sunday, 10 April, marking the start of the official celebrations of the fiftieth anniversary of the Rising. Enormous crowds gathered to watch the parade, lining the streets and, on O'Connell Street, the rooves of the buildings, including the GPO.

Another view of the parade taken from the roof of the Metropole cinema looking towards O'Connell Bridge.

12

Official Visits

Ireland was still a relatively new state in the scheme of things, having only become a full republic in 1949. Despite this there were a number of high-profile visits from foreign dignitaries throughout the 1960s. Here, His Excellency Mohammed Yousuf, the Pakistan Ambassador, inspects a guard of honour.

His Excellency Mohammed Yousuf being greeted by
President de Valera and Frank Aiken, Minister for External
Affairs, on 20 August 1962.

Just a month earlier, on 13 July, the same two Irish politicians, in slightly less formal attire, had met U Thant, the UN Secretary-General at Áras an Uachtaráin. U Thant became Secretary-General in late 1961 after the death of Dag Hammarskjöld, who was killed in a plane crash on the way to negotiate a ceasefire between UN troops and Katangese forces in the Congo.

On 22 August 1962 former US president General Dwight D. Eisenhower (*second from left*) touched down for a four-day visit to Ireland accompanied by his wife, Mamie, and their two grandchildren.
Included on his tour was a trip to Áras an Uachtaráin, where he
spoke with former Irish president Seán T. O'Kelly (*left*), President
de Valera and the Irish-American Ambassador, Matthew McCloskey.

Sinéad de Valera (*right*) regales Mamie Eisenhower (*centre*) and Mrs McCloskey with a story on the front lawn of the Áras.

JOHN
BARRY
UNITED STATES
NAVY

STAR OF THE MORNING GUIL

Above: The Eisenhowers split their time between Dublin, Wicklow and Wexford for the duration of their trip. This included a visit to the John Barry monument in Co. Wexford on 23 August 1962. General Eisenhower didn't seem to mind the bad weather, and neither did his grandchildren, David and Barbara Anne, standing to his left.

Left: Born in Wexford in 1745, John Barry was an officer in the Continental Army during the American Revolutionary War and later in the United States Navy. He is often referred to as 'The Father of the American Navy'. During the visit to the memorial, a guard of honour was formed by the local FCA (military reserves) for Eisenhower, who laid a wreath.

The General made time to inspect Irish Army troops during his visit.

He also visited his old friend Seán T. O'Kelly at his home in Roundwood, Co. Wicklow on 23 August. He travelled there in a UH-1 Iroquois 'Huey' helicopter, landing in the grounds of the residence.

A keen golfer, Eisenhower made sure he got the chance to play a round of golf at Portmarnock Golf Course. Here he tees off, watched by well-known amateur golfer Joe Carr (*first left*), among others.

The most high-profile foreign dignitary to touch down on Irish soil in the 1960s was, of course, President John Fitzgerald Kennedy, who landed on his ancestral soil on 26 June 1963. The welcome he received rivalled that of any of the decade's rock and roll gods. Thousands of people turned out at Dublin Airport to greet the US president as he arrived, and tens of thousands more swamped the city centre awaiting his motorcade. In this picture Kennedy gives his arm to a frail-looking President Éamon de Valera.

Waiting for the president. A young girl smiles in anticipation, holding the Irish and American flags as she waits for President Kennedy to drive past during his visit.

Huge crowds gathered at College Green (shown here) and elsewhere to watch President Kennedy's cavalcade pass on its way from the airport to the Irish president's residence. Irish and American flags, banners and bunting festooned the eight-mile route.

Parliament Street in Dublin came to a standstill as people gathered, eager to catch a glimpse of the president. A continual chorus of cheering and applause echoed across Dublin as Kennedy travelled through the city centre.

Crowds gathered everywhere President Kennedy went during his time in the country, many with American flags in hand.

The mood appears light-hearted as Kennedy stands in the Dáil for his address. During his speech, he made reference to the Irish Brigade which had fought on the Union side during the Civil War and presented the Dáil with one of the Brigade's flags 'in recognition of what these gallant Irishmen and what millions of other Irish have done for my country'. He went on to praise the role Ireland, despite being a small nation, was taking in the world and concluded: 'My friends, Ireland's hour has come. You have something to give to the world, and that is a future of peace with freedom.'

Kennedy was mobbed by journalists and fans alike during his four-day trip, which took him from Dublin to his family homestead in Dunganstown, Co. Wexford, from where his grandfather Patrick Kennedy had emigrated to America. From the rousing speeches he made during his tour of the country, to the grand receptions he was given at Áras an Uachtaráin and the poignant scenes as he greeted family at his ancestral home, these images capture a unique event in Irish history. Tragically just five months later, JFK would be dead.

In 1967 Jackie Kennedy, wife of the assassinated US president, visited Ireland with her children, Caroline and John. She declared on her arrival in Ireland: 'I am happy to be here in this land that my husband loved so much.' She is pictured here at her elegant best with Taoiseach Jack Lynch.

Like her husband, Jackie Kennedy was received at Áras an Uachtaráin by President and Mrs de Valera. Mrs Kennedy had come to Ireland to fulfil the wish of her husband, who had so enjoyed his trip in 1963 that he had vowed to return one day with his wife and children.